SHIT I
FORGOT
AGAIN

Shit I Forgot Again: Password Book With Tabs to Protect Your Usernames, Passwords and Other Internet Login Information | 6 x 9 inches

© 2019 Cover & Interior Design: Penny Quill

First Edition

Myrddin Publishing

unique electronic & print books

ISBN-13: 9781097276547

Published by
Myrddin Publishing Group

Contact us at:
https://www.myrddinpublishing.com
https://passwordkeeperbooks.com/

IMPORTANT, PLEASE READ

Are you always forgetting or losing your passwords? Are you worried about having a password organizer that screams "steal me" if you get burgled? Would you like a password book but you want something a little different?

If this sounds familiar, then this book was made for you. The cover is designed so it won't get noticed by opportunist thieves on the prowl who are looking for an obvious password logbook. It is also protected from online thieves by being a paperback.

Simply slip this volume into your bookshelf at home with your other books to hide it in plain sight.

There is a risk that if someone steals this or any other password keeper then they can get into your internet accounts. For this reason, please keep this book safe and secure and hidden at home.

To help you, this section shares tips for creating a secure password. This will make it difficult for anyone to get into your accounts even if they get this book.

Get a strong password

First of all, your password needs to be strong. Whatever you choose, there should be at least 8 characters in your password. If possible, these should be a mixture of lower and upper-case letters, numbers and special characters such as a $, *, &, @ etc.

You only need to remember half a password

The secret to using this book with this tip is that you only write down half of the password in this book. What you record needs to be random with a combination of characters. The reason that this method is secure is that half of the password is (only) stored in your head. It does not matter where you put the memorized half of the password into the

Create a Secure Password

Memorized half (only in your head):

wind

Random half (different each time and in this book):

Hydf54j@#f

Full password while logging in:

windHydf54j@#f

complete password. This can be at the beginning, middle or end, as long as it is not written down and is consistent so you remember it. The box above shows how this can work in practice.

As you can see this would be difficult to guess. You should not store it in an online password vault service unless you put it behind something protected by 2-step authentication.

Other ways to write down your password could be to use a code or have a theme but these can be very difficult to remember or will involve so much time to work it out that you will end up writing the real password anyway. With this method, you only need to remember the one 'password', albeit half a pass-

word but every password will still be different.

Make it even more secure

You can make this system even more secure by using the above method but to have different 'core' passwords for each type of website.

For example, you could have 'wind' for your bank, 'terrier' for shopping and other passwords for different websites. To make it easier to remember which password you have assigned to each website, replace the bulk of the password with stars, e.g. w**d and t*****r respectively. Using the password in the box above, these examples would become:

Bank password:

w**dHydf54j@#f

Shopping password:

t*****rHydf54j@#f

If anyone gets any one password it will not work for any other website so you will only need to change the one if it gets compromised.

2-step Verification

2-step verification/authentication is an extra step to make sure that access to your information, files and folders in an online service is restricted to you.

Instead of just relying on a password (which might be gained through nefarious means by hackers from a website or other ways), a second device is used which you always have on you such as a phone, tablet computer or key ring.

Using the 2-step verification method along with a secure password would mean any would-be infiltrator, bent on your destruction would need to have your password from this book, the memorized word from your mind AND your phone to gain access to your account.

This section talked about how to make storing passwords safer. The tips included were:

- have a different password for every website where you register,

- ensure that the password is strong with a good mix of letter, number and other characters,

- only write down part of your passwords (with clues so you that you can remember the other part and

- when you can, use 2 factor authentication.

I hope you will find these suggestions useful. If you like this book, I would be forever grateful if you could review it online and check out my other books. Safe Surfing!

AB

Site Name

Site Address

Username

Password

Email

Password hint

Pin

Notes

Site Name

Site Address

Username

Password

Email

Password hint

Pin

Notes

Site Name

Site Address

Username

Password

Email

Password hint

Pin

Notes

Site Name

Site Address

Username

Password

Email

Password hint

Pin

Notes

Site Name

Site Address

Username

Password

Email

Password hint

Pin

Notes

Site Name

Site Address

Username

Password

Email

Password hint

Pin

Notes

AB

Site Name

Site Address

Username

Password

Email

Password hint

Pin

Notes

Site Name

Site Address

Username

Password

Email

Password hint

Pin

Notes

Site Name

Site Address

Username

Password

Email

Password hint

Pin

Notes

Site Name

Site Address

Username

Password

Email

Password hint

Pin

Notes

Site Name

Site Address

Username

Password

Email

Password hint

Pin

Notes

Site Name

Site Address

Username

Password

Email

Password hint

Pin

Notes

Site Name

Site Address

Username

Password

Email

Password hint

Pin

Notes

Site Name

Site Address

Username

Password

Email

Password hint

Pin

Notes

Site Name

Site Address

Username

Password

Email

Password hint

Pin

Notes

Site Name

Site Address

Username

Password

Email

Password hint

Pin

Notes

Site Name

Site Address

Username

Password

Email

Password hint

Pin

Notes

Site Name

Site Address

Username

Password

Email

Password hint

Pin

Notes

Site Name

Site Address

Username

Password

Email

Password hint

Pin

Notes

Site Name

Site Address

Username

Password

Email

Password hint

Pin

Notes

Site Name

Site Address

Username

Password

Email

Password hint

Pin

Notes

Site Name

Site Address

Username

Password

Email

Password hint

Pin

Notes

Site Name

Site Address

Username

Password

Email

Password hint

Pin

Notes

Site Name

Site Address

Username

Password

Email

Password hint

Pin

Notes

CD

Site Name

Site Address

Username

Password

Email

Password hint

Pin

Notes

Site Name

Site Address

Username

Password

Email

Password hint

Pin

Notes

Site Name

Site Address

Username

Password

Email

Password hint

Pin

Notes

Site Name

Site Address

Username

Password

Email

Password hint

Pin

Notes

Site Name

Site Address

Username

Password

Email

Password hint

Pin

Notes

Site Name

Site Address

Username

Password

Email

Password hint

Pin

Notes

CD

Site Name

Site Address

Username

Password

Email

Password hint

Pin

Notes

Site Name

Site Address

Username

Password

Email

Password hint

Pin

Notes

Site Name

Site Address

Username

Password

Email

Password hint

Pin

Notes

Site Name

Site Address

Username

Password

Email

Password hint

Pin

Notes

Site Name

Site Address

Username

Password

Email

Password hint

Pin

Notes

Site Name

Site Address

Username

Password

Email

Password hint

Pin

Notes

Site Name

Site Address

Username

Password

Email

Password hint

Pin

Notes

Site Name

Site Address

Username

Password

Email

Password hint

Pin

Notes

Site Name

Site Address

Username

Password

Email

Password hint

Pin

Notes

Site Name

Site Address

Username

Password

Email

Password hint

Pin

Notes

Site Name

Site Address

Username

Password

Email

Password hint

Pin

Notes

Site Name

Site Address

Username

Password

Email

Password hint

Pin

Notes

CD

Site Name

Site Address

Username

Password

Email

Password hint

Pin

Notes

Site Name

Site Address

Username

Password

Email

Password hint

Pin

Notes

Site Name

Site Address

Username

Password

Email

Password hint

Pin

Notes

Site Name

Site Address

Username

Password

Email

Password hint

Pin

Notes

Site Name

Site Address

Username

Password

Email

Password hint

Pin

Notes

Site Name

Site Address

Username

Password

Email

Password hint

Pin

Notes

EF

Site Name

Site Address

Username

Password

Email

Password hint

Pin

Notes

Site Name

Site Address

Username

Password

Email

Password hint

Pin

Notes

Site Name

Site Address

Username

Password

Email

Password hint

Pin

Notes

Site Name

Site Address

Username

Password

Email

Password hint

Pin

Notes

Site Name

Site Address

Username

Password

Email

Password hint

Pin

Notes

Site Name

Site Address

Username

Password

Email

Password hint

Pin

Notes

Site Name

Site Address

Username

Password

Email

Password hint

Pin

Notes

Site Name

Site Address

Username

Password

Email

Password hint

Pin

Notes

Site Name

Site Address

Username

Password

Email

Password hint

Pin

Notes

Site Name

Site Address

Username

Password

Email

Password hint

Pin

Notes

Site Name

Site Address

Username

Password

Email

Password hint

Pin

Notes

Site Name

Site Address

Username

Password

Email

Password hint

Pin

Notes

Site Name

Site Address

Username

Password

Email

Password hint

Pin

Notes

Site Name

Site Address

Username

Password

Email

Password hint

Pin

Notes

Site Name

Site Address

Username

Password

Email

Password hint

Pin

Notes

Site Name

Site Address

Username

Password

Email

Password hint

Pin

Notes

Site Name

Site Address

Username

Password

Email

Password hint

Pin

Notes

Site Name

Site Address

Username

Password

Email

Password hint

Pin

Notes

EF

Site Name

Site Address

Username

Password

Email

Password hint

Pin

Notes

Site Name

Site Address

Username

Password

Email

Password hint

Pin

Notes

Site Name

Site Address

Username

Password

Email

Password hint

Pin

Notes

Site Name

Site Address

Username

Password

Email

Password hint

Pin

Notes

Site Name

Site Address

Username

Password

Email

Password hint

Pin

Notes

Site Name

Site Address

Username

Password

Email

Password hint

Pin

Notes

Site Name

Site Address

Username

Password

Email

Password hint

Pin

Notes

Site Name

Site Address

Username

Password

Email

Password hint

Pin

Notes

Site Name

Site Address

Username

Password

Email

Password hint

Pin

Notes

Site Name

Site Address

Username

Password

Email

Password hint

Pin

Notes

Site Name

Site Address

Username

Password

Email

Password hint

Pin

Notes

Site Name

Site Address

Username

Password

Email

Password hint

Pin

Notes

GH

Site Name

Site Address

Username

Password

Email

Password hint

Pin

Notes

Site Name

Site Address

Username

Password

Email

Password hint

Pin

Notes

Site Name

Site Address

Username

Password

Email

Password hint

Pin

Notes

Site Name

Site Address

Username

Password

Email

Password hint

Pin

Notes

Site Name

Site Address

Username

Password

Email

Password hint

Pin

Notes

Site Name

Site Address

Username

Password

Email

Password hint

Pin

Notes

GH

Site Name

Site Address

Username

Password

Email

Password hint

Pin

Notes

Site Name

Site Address

Username

Password

Email

Password hint

Pin

Notes

Site Name

Site Address

Username

Password

Email

Password hint

Pin

Notes

Site Name

Site Address

Username

Password

Email

Password hint

Pin

Notes

Site Name

Site Address

Username

Password

Email

Password hint

Pin

Notes

Site Name

Site Address

Username

Password

Email

Password hint

Pin

Notes

GH

Site Name

Site Address

Username

Password

Email

Password hint

Pin

Notes

Site Name

Site Address

Username

Password

Email

Password hint

Pin

Notes

Site Name

Site Address

Username

Password

Email

Password hint

Pin

Notes

Site Name

Site Address

Username

Password

Email

Password hint

Pin

Notes

Site Name

Site Address

Username

Password

Email

Password hint

Pin

Notes

Site Name

Site Address

Username

Password

Email

Password hint

Pin

Notes

Site Name

Site Address

Username

Password

Email

Password hint

IJ

Pin

Notes

Site Name

Site Address

Username

Password

Email

Password hint

Pin

Notes

Site Name

Site Address

Username

Password

Email

Password hint

Pin

Notes

Site Name

Site Address

Username

Password

Email

Password hint

Pin

Notes

Site Name

Site Address

Username

Password

Email

Password hint

Pin

Notes

Site Name

Site Address

Username

Password

Email

Password hint

Pin

Notes

IJ

Site Name

Site Address

Username

Password

Email

Password hint

Pin

Notes

Site Name

Site Address

Username

Password

Email

Password hint

Pin

Notes

Site Name

Site Address

Username

Password

Email

Password hint

Pin

Notes

Site Name

Site Address

Username

Password

Email

Password hint

Pin

Notes

Site Name

Site Address

Username

Password

Email

Password hint

Pin

Notes

Site Name

Site Address

Username

Password

Email

Password hint

Pin

Notes

Site Name

Site Address

Username

Password

Email

Password hint

IJ

Pin

Notes

Site Name

Site Address

Username

Password

Email

Password hint

Pin

Notes

Site Name

Site Address

Username

Password

Email

Password hint

Pin

Notes

Site Name

Site Address

Username

Password

Email

Password hint

Pin

Notes

Site Name

Site Address

Username

Password

Email

Password hint

Pin

Notes

Site Name

Site Address

Username

Password

Email

Password hint

Pin

Notes

IJ

Site Name

Site Address

Username

Password

Email

Password hint

Pin

Notes

Site Name

Site Address

Username

Password

Email

Password hint

Pin

Notes

Site Name

Site Address

Username

Password

Email

Password hint

Pin

Notes

Site Name

Site Address

Username

Password

Email

Password hint

Pin

Notes

Site Name

Site Address

Username

Password

Email

Password hint

Pin

Notes

Site Name

Site Address

Username

Password

Email

Password hint

Pin

Notes

KL

Site Name

Site Address

Username

Password

Email

Password hint

Pin

Notes

Site Name

Site Address

Username

Password

Email

Password hint

Pin

Notes

Site Name

Site Address

Username

Password

Email

Password hint

Pin

Notes

Site Name

Site Address

Username

Password

Email

Password hint

Pin

Notes

Site Name

Site Address

Username

Password

Email

Password hint

Pin

Notes

Site Name

Site Address

Username

Password

Email

Password hint

Pin

Notes

Site Name

Site Address

Username

Password

Email

Password hint

Pin

Notes

Site Name

Site Address

Username

Password

Email

Password hint

Pin

Notes

Site Name

Site Address

Username

Password

Email

Password hint

Pin

Notes

Site Name

Site Address

Username

Password

Email

Password hint

Pin

Notes

Site Name

Site Address

Username

Password

Email

Password hint

Pin

Notes

Site Name

Site Address

Username

Password

Email

Password hint

Pin

Notes

Site Name

Site Address

Username

Password

Email

Password hint

Pin

Notes

Site Name

Site Address

Username

Password

Email

Password hint

Pin

Notes

Site Name

Site Address

Username

Password

Email

Password hint

Pin

Notes

Site Name

Site Address

Username

Password

Email

Password hint

Pin

Notes

KL

Site Name

Site Address

Username

Password

Email

Password hint

Pin

Notes

Site Name

Site Address

Username

Password

Email

Password hint

Pin

Notes

Site Name
....
Site Address
....
Username
....
Password
....
Email
....
Password hint
....
Pin
....
KL Notes

Site Name
....
Site Address
....
Username
....
Password
....
Email
....
Password hint
....
Pin
....
Notes

Site Name
....
Site Address
....
Username
....
Password
....
Email
....
Password hint
....
Pin
....
Notes

Site Name

Site Address

Username

Password

Email

Password hint

Pin

Notes

Site Name

Site Address

Username

Password

Email

Password hint

Pin

Notes

Site Name

Site Address

Username

Password

Email

Password hint

Pin

Notes

Site Name

Site Address

Username

Password

Email

Password hint

Pin

Notes

Site Name

Site Address

Username

Password

Email

Password hint

Pin

Notes

Site Name

Site Address

Username

Password

Email

Password hint

Pin

Notes

Site Name
Site Address
Username
Password
Email
Password hint
Pin
Notes

Site Name
Site Address
Username
Password
Email
Password hint
Pin
Notes

Site Name
Site Address
Username
Password
Email
Password hint
Pin
Notes

Site Name

Site Address

Username

Password

Email

Password hint

Pin

Notes

Site Name

Site Address

Username

Password

Email

Password hint

Pin

Notes

Site Name

Site Address

Username

Password

Email

Password hint

Pin

Notes

Site Name
Site Address
Username
Password
Email
Password hint
Pin
Notes

Site Name
Site Address
Username
Password
Email
Password hint
Pin
Notes

Site Name
Site Address
Username
Password
Email
Password hint
Pin
Notes

Site Name

Site Address

Username

Password

Email

Password hint

Pin

Notes

Site Name

Site Address

Username

Password

Email

Password hint

Pin

Notes

Site Name

Site Address

Username

Password

Email

Password hint

Pin

Notes

Site Name

Site Address

Username

Password

Email

Password hint

Pin

Notes

Site Name

Site Address

Username

Password

Email

Password hint

Pin

Notes

Site Name

Site Address

Username

Password

Email

Password hint

Pin

Notes

Site Name

Site Address

Username

Password

Email

Password hint

Pin

Notes

Site Name

Site Address

Username

Password

Email

Password hint

Pin

Notes

Site Name

Site Address

Username

Password

Email

Password hint

Pin

Notes

Site Name

Site Address

Username

Password

Email

Password hint

Pin

Notes

Site Name

Site Address

Username

Password

Email

Password hint

Pin

Notes

Site Name

Site Address

Username

Password

Email

Password hint

Pin

Notes

Site Name

Site Address

Username

Password

Email

Password hint

Pin

Notes

OP

Site Name

Site Address

Username

Password

Email

Password hint

Pin

Notes

Site Name

Site Address

Username

Password

Email

Password hint

Pin

Notes

Site Name

Site Address

Username

Password

Email

Password hint

Pin

Notes

Site Name

Site Address

Username

Password

Email

Password hint

Pin

Notes

Site Name

Site Address

Username

Password

Email

Password hint

Pin

Notes

Site Name

Site Address

Username

Password

Email

Password hint

Pin

Notes

OP

Site Name

Site Address

Username

Password

Email

Password hint

Pin

Notes

Site Name

Site Address

Username

Password

Email

Password hint

Pin

Notes

Site Name

Site Address

Username

Password

Email

Password hint

Pin

Notes

Site Name

Site Address

Username

Password

Email

Password hint

Pin

Notes

Site Name

Site Address

Username

Password

Email

Password hint

Pin

Notes

Site Name

Site Address

Username

Password

Email

Password hint

Pin

Notes

OP

Site Name

Site Address

Username

Password

Email

Password hint

Pin

Notes

Site Name

Site Address

Username

Password

Email

Password hint

Pin

Notes

Site Name

Site Address

Username

Password

Email

Password hint

Pin

Notes

Site Name

Site Address

Username

Password

Email

Password hint

Pin

Notes

OP

Site Name

Site Address

Username

Password

Email

Password hint

Pin

Notes

Site Name
Site Address
Username
Password
Email
Password hint
Pin
Notes

OP

Site Name
Site Address
Username
Password
Email
Password hint
Pin
Notes

Site Name
Site Address
Username
Password
Email
Password hint
Pin
Notes

Site Name

Site Address

Username

Password

Email

Password hint

Pin

Notes

Site Name

Site Address

Username

Password

Email

Password hint

Pin

Notes

OP

Site Name

Site Address

Username

Password

Email

Password hint

Pin

Notes

Site Name

Site Address

Username

Password

Email

Password hint

Pin

Notes

Site Name

QR

Site Address

Username

Password

Email

Password hint

Pin

Notes

Site Name

Site Address

Username

Password

Email

Password hint

Pin

Notes

Site Name

Site Address

Username

Password

Email

Password hint

Pin

Notes

Site Name

Site Address

Username

Password

Email

Password hint

Pin

Notes

QR

Site Name

Site Address

Username

Password

Email

Password hint

Pin

Notes

Site Name

Site Address

Username

Password

Email

Password hint

Pin

Notes

Site Name

Site Address

QR Username

Password

Email

Password hint

Pin

Notes

Site Name

Site Address

Username

Password

Email

Password hint

Pin

Notes

Site Name

Site Address

Username

Password

Email

Password hint

Pin

Notes

Site Name

Site Address

Username

Password

Email

Password hint

Pin

Notes

QR

Site Name

Site Address

Username

Password

Email

Password hint

Pin

Notes

Site Name

Site Address

Username

Password

Email

Password hint

Pin

Notes

Site Name

Site Address

QR   Username

Password

Email

Password hint

Pin

Notes

Site Name

Site Address

Username

Password

Email

Password hint

Pin

Notes

Site Name

Site Address

Username

Password

Email

Password hint

Pin

Notes

Site Name

Site Address

Username

Password

Email

Password hint

Pin

Notes

QR

Site Name

Site Address

Username

Password

Email

Password hint

Pin

Notes

Site Name

Site Address

Username

Password

Email

Password hint

Pin

Notes

Site Name

Site Address

QR

Username

Password

Email

Password hint

Pin

Notes

Site Name

Site Address

Username

Password

Email

Password hint

Pin

Notes

Site Name

Site Address

Username

Password

Email

Password hint

Pin

Notes

Site Name

Site Address

Username

Password

Email

Password hint

Pin

Notes

QR

Site Name

Site Address

Username

Password

Email

Password hint

Pin

Notes

Site Name

Site Address

Username

Password

Email

Password hint

Pin

Notes

Site Name

Site Address

Username

ST

Password

Email

Password hint

Pin

Notes

Site Name

Site Address

Username

Password

Email

Password hint

Pin

Notes

Site Name

Site Address

Username

Password

Email

Password hint

Pin

Notes

Site Name

Site Address

Username

Password

Email

Password hint

Pin

Notes

ST

Site Name

Site Address

Username

Password

Email

Password hint

Pin

Notes

Site Name

Site Address

Username

Password

Email

Password hint

Pin

Notes

Site Name

Site Address

Username

ST

Password

Email

Password hint

Pin

Notes

Site Name

Site Address

Username

Password

Email

Password hint

Pin

Notes

Site Name

Site Address

Username

Password

Email

Password hint

Pin

Notes

Site Name

Site Address

Username

Password

Email

Password hint

Pin

Notes

ST

Site Name

Site Address

Username

Password

Email

Password hint

Pin

Notes

Site Name

Site Address

Username

Password

Email

Password hint

Pin

Notes

Site Name

Site Address

Username

ST

Password

Email

Password hint

Pin

Notes

Site Name

Site Address

Username

Password

Email

Password hint

Pin

Notes

Site Name

Site Address

Username

Password

Email

Password hint

Pin

Notes

Site Name

Site Address

Username

Password

Email

Password hint

Pin

Notes

ST

Site Name

Site Address

Username

Password

Email

Password hint

Pin

Notes

Site Name

Site Address

Username

Password

Email

Password hint

Pin

Notes

Site Name

Site Address

Username

ST

Password

Email

Password hint

Pin

Notes

Site Name

Site Address

Username

Password

Email

Password hint

Pin

Notes

Site Name

Site Address

Username

Password

Email

Password hint

Pin

Notes

Site Name

Site Address

Username

Password

Email

Password hint

Pin

Notes

ST

Site Name

Site Address

Username

Password

Email

Password hint

Pin

Notes

Site Name

Site Address

Username

Password

Email

Password hint

Pin

Notes

Site Name

Site Address

Username

Password

Email

UV

Password hint

Pin

Notes

Site Name

Site Address

Username

Password

Email

Password hint

Pin

Notes

Site Name

Site Address

Username

Password

Email

Password hint

Pin

Notes

Site Name

Site Address

Username

Password

Email

Password hint

Pin

Notes

UV

Site Name

Site Address

Username

Password

Email

Password hint

Pin

Notes

Site Name

Site Address

Username

Password

Email

Password hint

Pin

Notes

Site Name

Site Address

Username

Password

Email

Password hint

Pin

Notes

Site Name

Site Address

Username

Password

Email

Password hint

Pin

Notes

Site Name

Site Address

Username

Password

Email

Password hint

Pin

Notes

Site Name

Site Address

Username

Password

Email

Password hint

Pin

Notes

UV

Site Name

Site Address

Username

Password

Email

Password hint

Pin

Notes

Site Name

Site Address

Username

Password

Email

Password hint

Pin

Notes

Site Name

Site Address

Username

Password

Email

UV

Password hint

Pin

Notes

Site Name

Site Address

Username

Password

Email

Password hint

Pin

Notes

Site Name

Site Address

Username

Password

Email

Password hint

Pin

Notes

Site Name

Site Address

Username

Password

Email

Password hint

Pin

Notes

UV

Site Name

Site Address

Username

Password

Email

Password hint

Pin

Notes

Site Name

Site Address

Username

Password

Email

Password hint

Pin

Notes

Site Name

Site Address

Username

Password

Email

Password hint

Pin

Notes

Site Name

Site Address

Username

Password

Email

Password hint

Pin

Notes

Site Name

Site Address

Username

Password

Email

Password hint

Pin

Notes

Site Name

Site Address

Username

Password

Email

Password hint

Pin

Notes

UV

Site Name

Site Address

Username

Password

Email

Password hint

Pin

Notes

Site Name

Site Address

Username

Password

Email

Password hint

Pin

Notes

Site Name

Site Address

Username

Password

Email

Password hint

WX) Pin

Notes

Site Name

Site Address

Username

Password

Email

Password hint

Pin

Notes

Site Name

Site Address

Username

Password

Email

Password hint

Pin

Notes

Site Name

Site Address

Username

Password

Email

Password hint

Pin

Notes

Site Name

Site Address

Username

Password

Email

Password hint

Pin

Notes

Site Name

Site Address

Username

Password

Email

Password hint

Pin

Notes

Site Name

Site Address

Username

Password

Email

Password hint

WX

Pin

Notes

Site Name

Site Address

Username

Password

Email

Password hint

Pin

Notes

Site Name

Site Address

Username

Password

Email

Password hint

Pin

Notes

Site Name

Site Address

Username

Password

Email

Password hint

Pin

Notes

WX

Site Name

Site Address

Username

Password

Email

Password hint

Pin

Notes

Site Name

Site Address

Username

Password

Email

Password hint

Pin

Notes

Site Name

Site Address

Username

Password

Email

Password hint

WX Pin

Notes

Site Name

Site Address

Username

Password

Email

Password hint

Pin

Notes

Site Name

Site Address

Username

Password

Email

Password hint

Pin

Notes

Site Name

Site Address

Username

Password

Email

Password hint

Pin

Notes

WX

Site Name

Site Address

Username

Password

Email

Password hint

Pin

Notes

Site Name

Site Address

Username

Password

Email

Password hint

Pin

Notes

Site Name

Site Address

Username

Password

Email

Password hint

Pin

Notes

YZ

Site Name

Site Address

Username

Password

Email

Password hint

Pin

Notes

Site Name

Site Address

Username

Password

Email

Password hint

Pin

Notes

Site Name

Site Address

Username

Password

Email

Password hint

Pin

Notes

YZ

Site Name

Site Address

Username

Password

Email

Password hint

Pin

Notes

Site Name

Site Address

Username

Password

Email

Password hint

Pin

Notes

Site Name

Site Address

Username

Password

Email

Password hint

Pin

Notes

YZ

Site Name

Site Address

Username

Password

Email

Password hint

Pin

Notes

Site Name

Site Address

Username

Password

Email

Password hint

Pin

Notes

Site Name

Site Address

Username

Password

Email

Password hint

Pin

Notes

YZ

Site Name

Site Address

Username

Password

Email

Password hint

Pin

Notes

Site Name

Site Address

Username

Password

Email

Password hint

Pin

Notes

Site Name

Site Address

Username

Password

Email

Password hint

Pin

Notes

YZ

Site Name

Site Address

Username

Password

Email

Password hint

Pin

Notes

Site Name

Site Address

Username

Password

Email

Password hint

Pin

Notes

Site Name

Site Address

Username

Password

Email

Password hint

Pin

Notes

Site Name

Site Address

Username

Password

Email

Password hint

Pin

Notes

Site Name

Site Address

Username

Password

Email

Password hint

Pin

Notes

Site Name

Site Address

Username

Password

Email

Password hint

Pin

Notes

YZ

Site Name

Site Address

Username

Password

Email

Password hint

Pin

Notes

Site Name

Site Address

Username

Password

Email

Password hint

Pin

Notes

Site Name

Site Address

Username

Password

Email

Password hint

Pin

Notes

Site Name

Site Address

Username

Password

Email

Password hint

Pin

Notes

Internet Access Settings

Broadband Modem

Model
....
Serial Number
....
Mac Address
....
Admin URL/IP Address
....
WAN/IP Address
....
Username
....
Password
....
Notes
....

Router/Wireless Access
*Useful if you need to reset your router or wireless access

Model
....
Serial Number
....
Default Username*
....
Default Password*
....
Your URL/IP Address
....
Your Username
....
Your Password
....
Notes

WAN Settings

Mac Address
....
IP Address
....
Host Name
....
Domain Name
....
Subnet Mask
....
Default Gateway
....
DNS
....
Notes

LAN Settings

IP Address
....
Subnet Mask
....
DHCP Range
....
Notes

Wireless Settings

SSID
....
(Wireless name)
....
Channel
....
Security Mode
....
WPA Shared Key
....
WEP Passphrase
....
Notes

NETWORK
SETTINGS

Software Licenses

Software
....

License number
....

Purchased on
....

Notes

Software
....

License number
....

Purchased on
....

Notes

Software
....

License number
....

Purchased on
....

Notes

Software
....

License number
....

Purchased on
....

Notes

Software

License number

Purchased on

Notes

Software

License number

Purchased on

Notes

Software

License number

Purchased on

Notes

Software

License number

Purchased on

Notes

Software

License number

Purchased on

Notes

Notes